The Ecliptic

edited by

Richard

Owens

Flood

Editions

The Ecliptic

Joseph Gordon Macleod

Afterword copyright © 2016 by Richard Owens
Published by Flood Editions
www.floodeditions.com
ISBN 978-0-9903407-6-8
Design and composition by Quemadura
Printed on acid-free, recycled paper
in the United States of America
This book was made possible in part through
a grant from the Illinois Arts Council
The editor wishes to thank Andrew Duncan, James Fountain,
and Keith Tuma for their generous advice and assistance.

To Kit

this firstling of receptive marriage

Preface

All literature is born symbolic: but specific symbolism inside literature, if it is not a confession of a sleepy awareness, is at the best a technical fault. For a symbol, being an idea, should be allowed to develop as ideas do: but specific symbolism both in idea kills and mummifies its symbols once beyond the embryo, and in effect leads to as much tiresomeness in poetry as to hysterics in life. In this poem the symbols may seem strange: but this is because they play upon one another.

The poets of the day shrink from long poems not, as one critic thinks, from sensationalism, but partly because since the publication of the last important long poem, literary taste has learned and developed an easier, diffuse narrative, the novel, which has in its popular guise these advantages to an age of vulgar art, that it appears in a familiar form and can be an easy method of autobiographical indulgence: and partly, perhaps, because of this difficulty which symbolism encounters in any work longer than the instantaneous poem. I too would have written this poem by moments, had I been able. But its plan was too complex to pack into the comfortable upholstery of the studio chair. I was forced to build a house for it. If I have established but a small proportion of the meaning each week made more clear, my poem, though interest in it may be confined unhappily to few readers, will at any rate not have been unfruitful.

The following is a curt synopsis of the poem:

ARIES: Announces the principle of sacrifice upon which the child is offered: what matters to the child is sacrificed to what matters to others.

TAURUS: The inner purity, or understanding, the seed of which lies about to germinate in him, is sacrificed in his own mind to what he has been taught to consider matters more. The Goldfinch is an unintelligible voice whose authority the child recognizes with a romantic misunderstanding, but is made to reject: in which process he becomes standardized.

GEMINI: Conscious of loss by order of authority, he identifies this with the loss of his first passion, and finds it expressive of a general loss. This leads him to revolt against all control and authority, and so to destandardize himself at the cost of disintegrating himself.

CANCER: There is a phase in the twenties when this disintegration becomes almost complete. The will fails. The whole world seems to be a chaos of contradictory meaning without faith or effort.

LEO: Through succeeding years various attempts at redintegration are made. Prandial success is found to be spurious and vapid.

VIRGO: Physical union, if without unity on both sides, merely pleases one of the personal fragments, and is a succession of agreeable events connected by a false idealism.

LIBRA: Intellectual appreciation is a mere diæresis over the letter of things.

SCORPIO: Upon this dialectical superiority, or in Blake's word, Ratio, life with pain and illogicality turns, destroying it.

SAGITTARIUS: With the result that the divorced spirit, its seed still ungerminated, wanders through mystical and valueless faiths:

CAPRICORNUS: While the repressed energy of a life-time, working in subconscious moments and subconscious values, assumes control of the spiritual outlook, though with no outward effect:

AQUARIUS: By which time the will is too exhausted for assertion. The mind turns to contemplation of the past, and tries to justify itself by allocating responsibility elsewhere. Death ensues without conscious integration.

PISCES: But whether or not the 'individual' redintegrates himself, primal meaning and relation have existed, to which his endeavours contribute. Though he may not consciously enjoy, the potentiality subsists into posterity.

Each sign thus contributes to a single consciousness. Although I hope it will have significance for my time, this is not intended to be either a typical, or a unique, but merely a single, consciousness: nor to be the complete survey of a life, but merely a path through it. Many interconnections had to be omitted, others inserted as echoes, for conciseness. Again, I am not sure that we are all born with even the seed of this purity or understanding: and obviously some develop it, or receive it, in a more intense degree than others. However, to display this adequately, two signs had to be reserved, the first to introduce the new creation, the last to show its position when superficially finished. PISCES, then, shows this life against a background of Time, as the previous signs against Space. In the second place, the subject of the poem has put forth effort, which is indelible, whatever its value. The fact that his signs have existed, though disjunct, unifies them.

I preface with this synopsis because though aware that it exposes an author to misrepresentation of motive, even to animosity in certain quarters, myself I mistrust undue mystery in the philosophical or psychological aspects of poetry. To indicate (too briefly, indeed, but how otherwise in prose?) my purpose, which was neither moral nor argumentative, but simply poetic, is the only way I know of letting my readers judge whether that purpose is true or false, and its execution apt or unsuccessful.

July 1929

The Ecliptic

Aries, or, The Ram

The silence of the snow-turf has rooted itself in the terrain:
    Starved on the frozen stream wander the water-voles.
Earth is revoked. Withheld, the sky goes out in a purple
    Skeleton toga, brooched with embalmed pyramidal buds.
But that satin is winter-rubbed, those branches the tits have rifled:
    Now there is no new leaf turned by the zephyrs of green.
The wind is too stale to be young: the kiss of shrubs and sighing,
    Clockwise working like the cogwheels of the stars,
Obediently come to life like Japanese flowers in water,
    Missel-thrush to schedule mates, primroses rehearse,
Star-trained, without new endeavour of spring, wherein Procyon
    Touched and thrust in a first frenzy of absolute joy
A star-toccata freely. She is no autonomous mistress,
    Spring is caught in the law. Winter abides her king.

Over iced gravel the redbreast, as if from an aldered river,
    Adjusts his single and creaking reel invisible:

Plaintive the heifers lick the snow from bewildered muzzles
    Studying a white scene quaintly disconsolate.
Butcherboys, square-basketed, run to make warm their errands,
    Misogynist finches in drab clothes form bachelor clubs.
But all by order go, the judgment debtors of winter,
    All obediently. Winter abideth king.
Rime-salted boughs and friable tilth that make frost welcome
    So dupe with pretty promise our yet too long despair
That when at last wits fail for lack of honourable sunlight,
    Spring is anticipated honourable and fresh.
It comes. The frosts are gone. But impulsive purple and yellow
    Yet are slaves to the ground. When time folds over again,
Dire in the midst of lilies adored the disciplinary lily
    Hangs its head fulfilling the legal balances,
Not balances that embrace all, being all-comprehending;
    But balances that exclude, being but compromise.
Sap rises. The hedgehog wakes. Willow siphons explode effervescent
    Durable rockets feathering into durable stars.
A slow subfoliar boat, the hedgehog comes to the surface,
    The sap in the hazel climbs like water in a pump
Encroaching upon the soluble ice and outer coldness
    Forcing the catkins out to hang till they drop away.
Rhapsodize not: this ordered endeavour is yet the endeavour of engines
    Palpitating with noise of birds and motion of leaves:
Still the seasons fit their phrasing instruments together
    Apt to the notation. And winter still is king.

Stuffed is the cottage interior. Like Celtic legs and bodies
 Twines the furniture. Plushes, embroideries
Lap and rejoin. A breathlessness, a heat, envelops
 Flat surfaces, thick dust lit by a candle's light.
Envelops the flat surfaces, muffling the felt mattings,
 Warmth, vitality, enveloped in the dust.
Muffled like breath the air shifts, breath of the grandam sleeping
 Tactile, infrangible. Never the grandam snores.
Only time's passage, high above sights gauging, tautens
 February to February, roped from cot to grave.
  Such and so fleeting were our adult joys
  Which Time, or Sickness, speedily destroys.

Fragrant the Rose is, fragrant too a hand paternal
 Upon a cheek sun-hot, while fragrant hay
Merrily tosses, rabbits bounce, and cider in firkin
 Gurgles. *The Violet sweet:* blithe and creamed as a cheek
Maternal touched, when Spring comes homely, Spring demurely,
 And frivolous March gives birth irrepressibly.
White Lilies, cobras bewitched, *White Snow*, the silence-caster,
 As nightjars intrude upon the bleaching night——
'Won't this sampler be nice, Mama, when I've finished it?'
 . . . .

Throstles claypad their nests: the toad walks: lumbers
 After him the tortoise slow but businesslike.
Up and down elastic gnats jerk. The silver fishes

Swim on the wall while attendant weevil tramps the beam.
The wagtail, interpied, struts humouristic on the flagstones.
Spring at length homely, Spring demurely comes.

Now Sarah the Patriarch's wife, more than reproaches of women,
Feared and cultivated royal winter's reproach
As long astride of piaffing time in the way of a barren woman
As it had ceased to be after her manner with her,
And as sourly refusing to lose what spring she abandoned
Till the nine month miracle lept. Miracles die.
Like the rose's fragrance, whiteness of snow lilies,
Like joys at the touch of time or sickness, miracles die.
'Fragrant the Rose,' replied she, 'but as your grandmother wisely
Has written out for you, "is, but it fades in Time".'

Then, a blight on a bush, the hoarfrost covers the country.
Unbelted to time's wheels the girdling zodiac
Turns disconnected. Wood anemones obedient
Timebewildered search for a sign of the time in vain,
Crushed by the frostweight sink. The panting hedgehog abandons
His pursuit of game, and rolls himself to sleep
Again in the associate leaves of dead putrescent autumns:
Gnats wither and seedlings shrivel at early dawn.
Too early the chiff-chaff arrives, and the witchlike voice of the plover
Utters a ghostly shriek infirm on an empty field.
An hour-old songthrush taps from his egg an hour too early,

Its pliable bald pink skin, frozen to parchment, cracks.
Misgiven its mother machine, divorced of commanding currents,
    Deserts: and the apple blossom, brittle as porcelain,
Breaks. Then snow, that was once as warm as a woollen blanket,
    Cold as sheetsteel clamps the lifewarmth to the ground
Like armoured men that crush and smother a captured enemy's children
    Fiercely satisfying their cruel perverted lust.
And the noise of birds and the motion of leaves is stopped like an army.
    Straight without a snore the grandam drives to the grave
And so to the Ram at the outset was vernal sacrificing
    When the Lord saved Sarah from the reproach of her sex.

Now for the pressure of gales so firm are petioles shackled,
    Scarce they move in the flux, bound like the boy to the pyre,
Umbilically. Rooks are blown out of the sky. Like rubber
    Firs bend roaring. Wind drowns mice in the roof
And sparrows. The naked child squeals with terror, and freezing
    His fingers boneless fall into the palms of his hands
As he had them in the womb, when he sees his mechanical father
    Brandishing a knife in the holy ritual dance.
'Run this way,' said the Lord: 'Run that way,' said the Lord also:
    Both ways ran the father, and stopped, and saw the Ram.
Substitute no substitute he catches the ram in a thicket,
    Cuts the strings, and the child reels free no longer free.
The father binds the ram, and slaughters and burns its body
    A byword beacon for fathers both in and out of church.

The sermon ended, father and son go home to beef and potatoes.
  But Sarah stares in the fire. 'It is long,' she says in her heart,
'That he has not loved me so.' Scowling she lifts a hymnbook.
  'Take this, Isaac, to bed with you.' The miracle goes to bed.
'Learn hymn three-fourteen.' But because he had never been able
  To learn his hymns in bed, he carries the holy book
Up to the children's lavatory, and obedient tries as he sits there
  To engrave the word of the Lord, hymn three-fourteen, on his heart.

But month by century reappears in the windows of human museums
  A circular moon unheeded, because no planet is near,
By business hatted men. And month by month demanding
  Owl on finial sits, but nobody answers at all.
Like twelve leaves eddying pavane the constellations
  Leaves in the eddying dust, twelve on a circular wind,
Man like a stone in the middle. Seldom is there escaping
  So few ever grow up, or like to reply to the owl.
Night and day the filemot eddy turns: the crimson
  Leaf passes, stamped with Upsilon majescule.
The central stone is crushed: dust violets chokes and the roses,
  The stone deaf and blind, leaves not heard nor seen.
But the moon fronts the ram, a crescent to a crescent,
  The bruise purple-black upon her vernal brow.
The sampler has name and date, recording the hour when the throstle
  Died, and spring was smothered, and spring decayed.

Fragrant the Rose is, but it fades in Time,
The Violet sweet, but quickly past its Prime.
White Lilies hang their Heads, and soon decay
And whiter Snow in Minutes melts away.
Such and so withering are our early Joys
Which Time, or Sickness, speedily destroys.

Ann Annall

August 20, 1806

Aged 12 Years.

Taurus, or, The Bull

'Goodly bull, come, Hero Dionysus,
To Elaeans' shrine, a pure shrine, pounding
Oxhoof graced, Goodly Bull, O Goodly
Bull,' so to herself hummed exiled Pyrrha
Pent in sorry school in ugly Scyros,
While about the Sporades sunblasted
In the Icarian Sea the pallid seagulls
Wait on level ropes, upbobbing mastheads,
Roofranks pantile-spaced, or in the cobalt
Sea parabolas describing useless
Pass the time, as waterdrops dispearled by
Boys revolving kettles. Cormorants dully
Dive for lack of better occupation.
And the wind drops, so that the deaf girls murmur
'Quiet the noon is,' though intense maynoises
Roar, the air is cleft with tune and passage,
Blackbird, dragonfly, finches, lark and blackcap,

Beetle and bee: and blue on a violet cable
Where sky sea meets speeds the keen kingfisher.
Factory noonblast wails like startled peewits
Sudden upon the planes of expectation,
Then recloses as before expectant.
Pale figsuckers spirt. The longlapped Grecian
Waves scarce tip the lullable lying wherries:
All again expectant through the meantime
Wing and sing, unconscious what approaches.
Forced is Dolopian silence in the convent,
Diet of pulse and aggregate of lentils,
Or, inept, else provender of schoolgirls'
Giggling repartee not quite unseemly,
Sporad stones a girl leaps over never.
So to herself was thinking exiled Pyrrha
Pent in sorry school in ugly Scyros.

      Honey jenneting
          hyaline early to graft to zircon
             a filemot
                reedpipe stonepine Akanthis begins
     with a tiffany
        homily easy to learn to listen
           in aphetic
              stonepine goldfinch Akanthis sings

Easy to learn to listen to lilliput trebles,
Scarletfaced Akanthis, easy minstrel:
Pyrrha learns your rapid Hellenic gospel
Swift as the last forerunner of Aurora
Ere herself come welcome on cold of morning,
Learns she. Early to graft to cinnabar apples
Hesperid gems of sap and silica—Goodly
Bull, O Goodly Bull, release your rapture.
Into the winejars like a cistern filling
Liberate your dithyrambic wisdom
Till myself have life and understanding,
Charging, enlarging, till with Pramnian softness
Amphoræ as big as vats are brimming.
So shall Iris finish her opalfiring
Starchameleons. So come Dionysus.

But the flagstones in the house quadrangle
Echo the hockey team, o'erhot as Thracian
Soldiers, and with bad Dolopian tempers.
——Hallo, Pyrrha, looking mouldy——Rudely
Eager for comfort, fill baths, strip their sweaters,
Stand resentful.
          ——'tever do you think a-
  'Bout, you Pyrrha?
        Studying βουφονία

——Studying what?

        The sacrifice at Athens.

——'tever's that?

        Not know it? Well then listen,

Daughters of Lycomêdês (thus to address them

With respect that's no respect) I'll tell you.

        Once every year Zeus Polios's altar is

        Got ready for the harvest, on the Acropolis,

        To win the favour of the God of Crops. They bake

——Who do?——Priests, I suppose——a sort of farl or cake

        Of wheat and barley, stuff that only the bulls could eat

——What bulls?——The sacred bulls——indeed? but if there's wheat

  What are the bulls for? Isn't wheat sacred?

                    They're to enable

        Priests to choose oblation for God Vegetable,

        Driving them round and round the altar, till one stops

        To eat, which shows he's chosen by the God of Crops:

        Then all the rest are driven away. ——A silly scheme!

What happens if two stop?——Don't interrupt, eupheme.

        Let me go on.——Yes let the poor thing tell her tale,

She's mad and mouldy.——Girls bring water in a pail

        And two men step up with an axe and knife in hand.

        These they wash in the water. Then they go and stand

        Up to the bull, but both prepared to run away

        Immediately they've done. The first one, Butcher A,

Fells the bull with the axe, and soon as it is down,

Drops axe and takes to his heels, as if he were a clown

With harlequin's hot poker at him. Meanwhile Butcher B,

The knife one, hurriedly slits its throat, yells as if he

Too were being left behind by God, lets knife

Fall, and is off, no one knows where, to save his life.

So the bull's slain, fit offering, deed unfit,

And no one's left to be responsible for it.

——What rot! Who told you that?

                    My Uncle Calchas.

——And him?——Poor poop, her ruddy uncle Calchas!——

Authority upon the *Βουφονία*

——Upon the what? Bou-how much?

                 ——*Βλυφωνία*

I think she said——I said——The *Βουβωνία*——

——No, *Βουφαλλία*——I said——O these juvencle

Uncles!——You sin too much, that's what it is.

Do tell us what's the matter with you, Pyrrha,

Always mouldy?

                  Yes, for youth, the longer

Like cheese you keep it, more thereby encrust it

Moulds of the island air.——They dim and snigger.

Water drains off sucking like drenched clayfields.

O irritating wet of adolescents.

Thistle virelay
    thalamus empty to freeze to winter
       an echo of
          goldfinch reedpipe Akanthis wins.

When I shall die, this finch shall epitaph me:
Pyrrha, alive, loved the goldfinch's song:
The girl is dead: the goldfinch still is singing.
Ah yes, here wins indeed the rilling goldfinch
Over black dreams that from the strumming hollies
Spill like ouzelsong: over Athênê
Polias starting in the house quadrangle
Like a statue, pale as pugilistic
Moon above, though smudged her rounded forehead.
Iô, Iô, for the coming of Dionysus!
Like a cockchafer planing through a window
Glints the dagger in the silks electric.
Pyrrha prepares. Her hundred nightmares addle.
Iô, Iô, the holiday of harvest
Pyrrha's day dawns, crops of long rehearsal.
Wash well the blade, Ulyssês, in the water,
Purely. As for you, redfaced Akanthis,
Go serenade recumbency's sow-thistles
Scabby cowdung in the marly barley.
Go serenade dogroses, whose pink petals

Open to pretty songs. Could rilling goldfinch
Unbruise Selênê's bruises by his easy
Music? No, he wins not. That bird gospel,
Fancy it was, and when a blade is dawning,
Fancy no light has. Strike, long wanted dagger,
Strike at the dewlap stupid as limp leather.
Cunning the cut: the gods will smile approving.
What do they say? I, run? What are they saying?
Pyrrha has slain the goodly Dionysus?
Meaning that bull? There never was such coming:
For, see, the amphorae are dry and empty
When you unseal them. Would you avenge on Pyrrha?
Was't I that slew? Nay, but the dagger did it.
Was my name Pyrrha?

                              Now it is Achillês.

Gemini, or, The Twins

Flow full, Eurôtas river, we hymn Castor dead.
Flow from your fond Borêan watershed
Alone to wide ship-bare Laconian bight.
You almost are Arcadian, sprang to light
A few miles from that Paradisal border,
Mapped out for all eternity, by order
Of a moment: yes eternally removed
From such a country as you might have grooved
Luxuriantly. But languish not to alter,
Where to fantasticise would be to falter,
To falter weakly, unachieving change.
Flow full through the commercial counties strange
And hostile, which your tributaries shred;
Flow full, Eurôtas river, we hymn Castor dead.

To Polydeucês dead, if not to other,
A double star, that beautifies his brother,

Tyndarid dot of lustre doth he grow

Among the crooked archipelago,

A Common Castor, open to the days.

But that companion who was ἀιτής

Hearkening to Polydeucês' word,

Now hears no more, and is no more preferred

As I preferred him to the world's successes,

And joins no more in baffled anxious stresses,

And no more in the flutesound slyly weaves

About his bulwarks snakes and ivyleaves

And no more blows dark bubbles in the vine,

Nor comes long waited to th'Elaean shrine,

That pure shrine, pounding on his hoofs of bull.

Eurôtas river, un-Arcadian, flow full,

For we hymn Castor dead.

                But do you flow

So conscious, and of rout decupled so,

As, when through commonplace and empty meads

Your unromantic sad routinist leads,

Too high your rarities you may not prize,

Nor sob for excellencies otherwise:

As, when in hope the craft you circumvent

Of Lycomêdês that grim government,

Who killed my Castor, though his body still

Circles the sky impossible to kill,

You that authority may drown completely,

Down him and drown him, who as state-discreetly

Laid Castor low and bruised again the moon

A second blow both in an afternoon.

All autocrats must perish, grand or mean.

Who worst conspires against his king or queen

Loves best his land. Those patriot politicians,

Heroes to sublimate their own ambitions,

Are like their enemies mere meretricians.

Drown, drown them all. Such gurgles will be good.

That free may float the rights of brotherhood

Along, from your not quite Arcadian spring,

An interracial peace. And flowering

And pure and fruitening and grand

For those who can, will and dare understand,

May adult wholeness rise, and freedom burst,

Unhindered. Those dour moralists who first

Were timorous, shall timorous again

Leave well alone to what could ne'er attain

Their wan misunderstanding: and sad Sin,

Exiled to lawcourt and teatable din,

No more lie, where it not belongs, in bed.

Flow full, Eurôtas river, we hymn Castor dead.

Flowers with clients in the end of May
Preserve his pollened youth, night and/or day
Open to show winged curio-fanciers
As I do my spring-animafacture, theirs.
The mauve-polled knapweed, as unkempt as he,
The woolly willowherb of Therapnê,
Remind each other where sun-currents meet.
Still from the hedge hangs purple bittersweet
Its deadly double moments of desire.
Sudden as ever in the gloomy mire
Shouts scarlet and released the pimpernel:
Green pentahedral moschatel,
It knew him well.
Ai, ai! The purple iris, once in Greece
Hyacinth-born, laments our broken peace,
The youth shed in our limbenlacing havens.
With red are tinged the lemon water avens,
With red the vipers-bugloss ere the hot
Adult June bakes it, still erythroglot,
Bluely: and eyes, as pricked and blurred as these,
See blood upon the cubed fritillaries,
And clotted blood upon the yarrow head.
Flow full, Eurôtas river, we hymn Castor dead.

The nightingale that spluttered in the spring
Now dry of throat is harshly gurgling
His evening answer to the cuckoo's curt
Self-pitying complaint of annual hurt.
Flowers that syndically mate in May
Become rubescent roots, to our dismay,
Of grisly yews in crowded burial grounds.
While we, in whose deaf ears alarum sounds
Already, are seen hankering after bones
And disappearances and monotones,
Clad in death's decency as of old in flesh's
Beauty private in its rayon meshes.

Though we have laid no foreheads on a sheet
Kissing the stiffness of cold face and feet,
Yet we have known a stiffness worse than this,
Of new cold sheets where there is none to kiss.
Old smells of ancient eaten growth: wormrotten
Hollowness of abandoned aims: stalecotton
Cerecloths that wrap embraces long forbidden:
Parthenic rapture crudely chapped and chidden:
Acquaintance like a woman's womb steeltrodden
Dumbed, made abortive: and inside, the sodden
Slimy ort of what had once been self.

So the first coffin heartward to the shelf
Is lifted. So death's children threnoded.
Flow full, Eurôtas river, we hymn Castor dead.

We may have lost him. Our deeds have not died,
Nor our nude purposes that side by side
Spouted our vigorous ambitions each.
Then shall, like turtledove on bough of beech,
I Polydeucês sit without a stir
Making flat forenoon solitarier?
Or people youth with fancy's pastoral fleece
And scented homosexual ghosts of Greece?
Up, Polydeucês: turn this prurient Pnyx,
But not by studio turns nor schoolgirl tricks,
Into Panathêneia, that supreme——
No carnival, no academic dream——
But a further aim, a call, that chief
Of clarions, a delectable belief.
Such is the fruit the nymphs of Nysa fed.
Flow full, Eurôtas river, we hymn Castor dead.

(But Hêra who the Bacchic god deranged
Seeing this Polydeucês so estranged
From government and business, him drove,
An intellectual shepherd in a grove

Unlearned planted, through a London park
To drown his loneliness in deeds of dark,
Where bourgeoise Muses, where suburban Nymphs
Apollo's ichor fighting vaccine lymphs,
With close-pulled clothes along the Serpentine
Undulate haunches, as of mares, in line.
King Lycomêdês with a big cigar
Beacons from the abode where the infernal are.
But we're no fools. Rational and astute
Walks Polydeucês with a prostitute.
They take a taxi. Festival is fled.
Full flows the river. Castor lieth dead.)

Oimoi. Who killed him? Half the double star
Harkens to end its earthly avatar.
Aided by nymphs and such maternal muses
Shall on himself avenged be Polydeucês.
Thus the survivor of the Gemini
Mourns, to explore futile futurity.

Cancer, or, The Crab

Moonpoison, mullock of sacrifice,

Suffuses the veins of the eyes

Till the retina, mooncoloured,

Sees the sideways motion of the cretin crab

Hued thus like a tortoise askew in the glaucous moonscape

A flat hot boulder it

Lividly in the midst of the Doldrums

Sidles

The lunatic unable to bear the silent course of constellations

Mad and stark naked

Sidles

The obol on an eyeball of a man dead from elephantiasis

Sidles

All three across heaven with a rocking motion.

The Doldrums: 'region of calms and light baffling winds near Equator.'

But the calms are rare

The winds baffling but not light

And the drunken boats belonging to the Crab Club

Rock hot and naked to the dunning of the moon

All in the pallescent Sargasso weed

And windbound, seeking distraction by the light of deliverance

For

What are we but the excrement of non-existent noon?

    (Truth like starlight crookedly)

What are we all but 'burial grounds abhorred by the moon'?

And did the Maoris die of measles? So do we.

But there is no snow here, nor lilies.

The night is glutinous

In a broad hearth crisscross thorn clumps

Smoulder: distant fireback of copse

Throws back silence: glassen ashes gleam in pond

The constellations which have stopped working (?)

Shimmer. No dead leaf jumps.

On edge of lawn a glowworm

Hangs out its state-recognized torchlamp

Blocks of flowers gape dumb as windows with blinds drawn

And in the centre the rugate trees

Though seeming as if they go up in smoke

Are held like cardboard where they are.
Bluehot it is queer fuel to make the moon move.

Agesias said: 'Nero was an artist because he murdered his mother
Sensibility (subliminal) is of more importance than moral obligation
      (prandial).'
  But Agesias paints cottages in watercolours and fears his own mother.
Barbarieus said: 'I am passionately in love with Gito who spurns me for
      Praxinoê'
  But until he saw them together he was merely disturbed by Gito's
      eyelashes.
Galônus said: 'The subsequent shrivelling of an orchid doesn't alter the
      value of its beauty.'
Decanus said: 'Joy in nothing. Either dies joy or what produced it.'
  But Galônus is attractive to women, Decanus obese, poor, obtuse.
Epinondas said: 'I have been a liar, now no longer so.'
Zeuxias said: 'What I have always been, I shall remain, a fool.'
  Is it better to be self-deceived or lazy?
Epator was drunk for two days: Theodorus traced his disease to college,
      Iphogenês saw God and died,
And so down the Alphabet, aye, and the Persian,
With variegated gutturals and sibilants, the Gaelic with diphthongs and
      triphthongs,
Choctaw with three different clicks
Each letter is somebody

But the Crab is nobody

Nobody

Nobody

A ganglion of neurotic imitations

Composed of each letter in turn

Jointed by conflicts he does not want

A word that never existed with a sense nobody can understand.

Suffering for the sins his father refuse to commit

He sits and thinks about the twiddling toes of Gunerita

A boy-girl or girl-boy of an average pulchritude

Haunted by phantoms of his female self

Whom he has never seen but composed himself, thus:

    Breasts of Augustina brains of Beatrice

    Arms of Capucine on the motherliness of Dorothea

    Eyes of Evelyn in the brow of Francesca

    Fragrance of Gretchen with the understanding of Helen

This he desires, but despises:

Bhah!

Always sideways, crabs walk.

Either he is not fit for this world

Or this world not fit for him. But which?

After all this pain of development is there neither interval nor reward?

They lured him with promises,

Now it has all slipped sideways

What is the good, I ask you, of going into a melting-pot
If fated to melt again after getting out of it?
The answers are: He is not out of it
Determined to budge not from yon slippery rock
Not a yard, no, nor an inch, no, nor a barleycorn's breadth
For Chance is not blind but unimpedable
And we call it blind because
Since we frustrate it only by chance
We prefer to shut our own eyes.

The crab however crawls on.

He must therefore be a crab subnormal.
One day, one of his foreclaws, assembled as usual by many men,
Being longer than the other, turns and pinches his tentacles
With the other he pinches the persons that assembled the long one
Next day the short one, equally alien, is the longer
And the process is reversed.
In mass production one hand never knows
The evil the other is inspiring it to do
This is a heretic even to the faiths he fails to believe
So worthless, awkward, unintelligible,
The crab crawls on.

He has suffered because he was ugly

Let him be cruel now that he is attractive

Caring not whether he fructifies cruelty or is merely hard on self.

We trap our goldfinch trapping our souls therewinged

Sacrifice our mad gods to the madder gods:

We hymn the two sons of Leda and Zeus Aegis-bearer

We don't. We drink and drivel. My

    poor Catullus, do stop being such a

    fool. Admit that lost which as you watch is

    gone. O, once the days shone very bright for

    you, when where that girl you loved so (as no

    other will be) called, you came and came. And

    then and there were odd things done and many

    which you wanted and she didn't not want.

    Yes indeed the days shone very bright for

    you. But now she doesn't want it.

                            Don't you either,

    booby. Don't keep chasing her. Don't live in

    misery, carry on, be firm, be hardened.

    Goodbye, girl: Catullus is quite hardened,

    doesn't want you, doesn't ask, if you're not

    keen—though sorry you'll be to be not asked.

    Yes, poor sinner . . . what is left in life for

    you? Who'll now go with you? Who'll be attracted?

Whom'll you love now? Whom say you belong to?

Whom'll you now kiss? Whose lips'll you nibble?

—Now you, Catullus! you've decided to be hardened.

How can I be hardened when the whole world is fluid?

O Aphroditê Pandêmos, your badgers rolling in the moonlit corn

Corn blue-bloom-covered carpeting the wind

Wind humming like distant rooks

Distant rooks busy like factory whirring metal

Whirring metallic starlings bizarre like cogwheels missing teeth

These last grinning like the backs of old motor cars

Old motor cars smelling of tragomaschality

Tragomaschality denoting the triumph of self over civilization

Civilization being relative our to Greek

              Greek to Persian

              Persian to Chinese

Chinese politely making borborygms to show satisfaction

Satisfaction a matter of capacity

Capacity not significance: otherwise with an epigram

Epigrams—poems with a strabismus

Strabismus being as common spiritually as optically the moon

The moon tramping regular steps like a policeman past the houses of the
      Zodiac

And the Zodiac itself, whirling and flaming sideways

Circling from no point returning through no point
Endlessly skidding as long as man skids, though never moving,
    Wavers, topples, dissolves like a sandcastle into acidity.

Is there nothing more soluble, more gaseous, more imperceptible?
Nothing.

Leo, or,
The Lion

The crab that crept upon the twins and bull
Has sidled off, and all is fluxion. Now the Lion stalks
The Ghost of Dionysus rendered animal,
Lashing majestic graces as he walks
Plumb in the centre of the Amphitheatre.
Lightnings flash and crumble, but as yet no thunder comes,
Nor peapod rain
To spoil his wavy mane,
He is too capable,
Too confident to be undignified.
The mighty crowd proclaims him potentate,
Throne, Princedom and Dominion, Virtue, Power,
Who fills their little interests for an hour
For them to throw their hats up, roar, and anxiously subside.

Now but the bookies' voices bless
His coming for their business.

Standeth he still and glowers
All four feet firm on sand,
Like waterspouts, like factory towers,
Flatness to flatness mounting, and
His tail brooming anger
Like coloured atmosphere before a storm.

Now he goes on intent,
Low as a king-snake glides,
Slow as a snake that hides,
Neck from shoulders bent,
Head like a lamp alert,
Then he stops on the scent
All four feet on the sand,
Growling and growling.

Then with a rush the storm breaks into battle.
Dust chokes his eyes and throat
Turning his leonine roar to a rattle;
He is tumbled about
Like a little boat,
Loins and back buffeted, he is thrown out.
His muffled breathing from the blanket he withdraws
Sits on his haunches like a cat:
Then rises and crouches,
Crouches and springs, he knows not what at,

With glaring fangs and cusping claws
Into the dust and the darkness
Prowling and prowling.

And then a battle royal is started,
A lion and a thunderstorm:
The lion blind, the enemy dumb,
Vaguely shaped as electric-hearted
Fires sway in the northern scene.
Heat and daydust of summer landscape,
As brides in a bridebed lie and wonder,
Are ready to give themselves to thunder.
But the lion treads them to a morass,
A tawny force on a tawny mass,
Rolling on his adversary's noise,
Invisible, intangible, infrangible.

Then he again recoils to rest:
But lightning cleaves the clouds, reveals
As dappled light a hidden nest,
His challenging opponent: whom to see
The lion springs to conflict angrily.

The huge machine of battle is engaged
Whose every gesture is assessed and paged,

The referee is put into commission
And every payment has its right position.
The unwheeled currents run from term to term,
Blue sparks ignite, zinc cells eject their sperm,
Short seeds of sound pop like gorsepods at noon,
Like plectrums plucking at the fluid tune.
Sustained vibrating in the bearingcase,
Pulsation conjures down the driving race
A tree of wires and thumping cylinders;
An oily wheel obediently whirrs;
And right along the tubes and branches goes
A white hot sap sucked from the dynamos.
Far from the popping of the summer pods
In a hot chamber the eccentric rods
Check their rotation and rotate again
Shifting positions like machines in pain.
Further, and hotter yet, the great pipe spires
Fearfully toasted in the furnace fires:
And men like measures peep through seablue glass
To regulate the universal farce.
Thus organized and tested and assessed
The warfare follows on the routine rest.

But now the dynamite explodes.
The glass sky cracks, lead cargoloads

Collapse in fragments on the scena:

The heat rips like cloth:

And accumulated thunder tumbles and bubbles cool across the arena.

The lion shakes the sweatdrops from his ears

And redirects his magicbound careers,

Whence the first flash came.

Raindrops begin to fall, dropped watery daisies

In a brief meadow, ere the peal

Of thunder passes.

Lightning makes a vapid flame

Unanswered in the ever-rising hum

Of distant downpours, like vibrating finger-glasses.

Already it is cooler. Breezes from the hill

Make the grass and bushes black and green.

The dust is laid, and the wet sand is clean:

The lion waits for revelation still.

Sudden and instantaneous lightning fills

The assembled airs,

And joyful thunder romping down the stairs

Enfranchises the echoes of the hills.

At last the watchful lion sees

Small as a sparrow in the anonymities

The enemy as human: darts at him,

Swift as a hawk that plunges past a tree,

And bears him to the ground, his claws
Fix on him, an acre-ton of power
Crushes him, his jaws
Open to roar his triumph and devour——

When suddenly all purpose and desire
Vanish like matchflame in a broader fire,
And all the want that fills his aching head
Is to return, to drink, to go to bed.
Wherefore he turns, oblivious of the yells
Desiderative employers and pert damosels
(With similar intents) direct at him;——
If he is Lion, he has Lion's whim.——
Yet not forgetting manners due to friends
Nor due successes honorarium,
He bows the compass of the auditorium,
And walks away. And so the contest ends.
But on return from working for his keep
What else has he to do, save eat and sleep?

Virgo, or,
The Virgin

'A wooden nuthatch taps my girdled womb,'
The Virgin called, 'as brittle now as ivywood.
When I the bridegrowth part toward the pines,
Woodpecker in triforium derides
With instant yell: at which the woodsmoke trembles
Loitering like a trespasser. The embers
All fall pale. And sight deserts mine eyes.'

'I am here, here,' came Leo's answering cry,
'Here where the wren is faltering in his song,
Here where the brushwood parts, and burning logs
Fill the live wood with incense of destruction.
Fear no woodpecker, but be full of courage:
Soon shall our tangents meet.'
                                        The hours wore on
Till closer called the Virgin to her man,
'Are you there? there?' 'Where quivers this spruce fir.'

'Already I can see the sunset air
Like a long goldfish under weeds of branches.'
'Then we are not far off.' The evening dances
On and on. Unseen from up behind
A primrose moon splashes the open pines
They make for. The toy stars begin their play.
Then calls the Virgin tremulously again,
'A wooden nuthatch taps me. O, I fear.'
Which Leo answers, 'I am almost there.'
His very gentleness makes her more frightened
As if a storm crooned cradlesong, or lightning
Fingered. But she calms her face and hands
Proceeding, till the birchfrustration ends.

Her lover catches her, and over dust
White sand dust soft as carpets costliest,
They walk the heath, and listen to the night.
Electric nightjars, hither-thither wired,
Whirr bells from east to west and west to east:
The nearer moths zip at the lower leaves,
Breezes stuffed in little wings: and the winds puff
Exotically with smell of pines and earth.
Beyond the hill, two dogs bark: a forlorn goat
Croaks with despair: and down the London road
White beams of motor cars that flash in suite
Continual radii, dip and reappear.

Now is the hour of which the witch has spoken
When from the dross shall lie apart the golden:
Now is the hour, Leo, to dismiss
The spell that binds her, burst the chrysalids,
Glued girdle. Let the summer be achieved,
Let dragonflies go glittering from the reeds.

He turns to take her. But before he reaches,
She springs away, a bleating ram, a creature
Frightened, and upturns her pleading face,
'Rather turn yourself to a man,' it cries. Amazed,
He follows near. Whereat the curving horns
Shoot out, as wicked as a bull that gores,
And her eyes glare with savage purpose. Hate
Tosses her as she paws the ground: and faint
With wilderment as he stands apart,
'Rather turn yourself to a man,' it lows afar.
Made yet and yet more virile he strides on
Lassoing her with love: but all too soon
At his approach (as a moth's wing-beat quickly)
He drawing near observes the bullock dwindling
Into a rotting corpse of lost acquaintance,
In whose liquescent lips the cackle straightens
Hard and dry: 'Rather turn yourself to a man.'

'A man, man am I,' he retching stands
And sobs: whereat the corpse gurgles again
And shivers. He puts out a hand and waits.
Then while the yaffle yells demoniac laughter,
A loathsome crab it sidles cold and crafty
And 'Rather turn yourself to a man' diminutive
It hisses swan-vindictively at him.

Thereafter baffled silence mutes the heath,
Subdues the garish gorses with its breath,
And reigns moon-equal on the fusted heather.
He now too puzzled to pursue the game
Awaits her next move. This she does not make.

As a child's brain, born whole but prematurely
Might in a month have worked to standard duly,
But that month missing long as it survives
Lags from itself a month or more behind,
So the lost lover cannot understand
By what lack yet she sees him not a man
And gropes. But nature heedless presses on,
And oversoon the invisible marching sun
Flashes to Spica in the Virgin's heart,
Who, the word catching, ere he moves a yard
Vibrates to ecstasy on highest string

A note that throbs among the Seraphim.

The unicorns that nose about the door

Fling up their heads to hear it, and with horn

And hoof batter to enter: some to the back

Gallop to rescue: others mount the tank

Below the window and attack the glass:

And others round and round the cottage race

Looking for weaker openings. Stays a pause

As if preparing for a final chord.

And then the Virgin cries.

At which sharp anguish like the crack of ice

All that was firm gave way. The moonlit night

Pitching as on a wave, the waters broke

Splashing their sweetness on the midnight rocks.

Over the tree-crests like a flock of finches

Darted and swooped exquisite joys and prickings

And tiny silver pain like that of fainting.

The sky spread broad with sudden glow of paining,

Then closed to darkness and the echoing

Of the fleet hooves of the sad fugitive

Unicorns, defaulting unicorns,

Upon the road. As they went, upward soared

A nearer echo that increased in power,

From a rough movement as of boys that ride

Unsure, to subtler motion, harmonied:
Now with increased hope, now with certitude,
As from far copses beaters' cries are tuned
Faintly but firmer as the birds approach.
Faintly but firmer sound the tended hopes
And with approaching knowledge every nerve
Kindles and every fold and bank is stirred,
Till the old radiance glares, and pain is drowned
In joy that floods through all the roads and towns
Turning the people out in holiday.

Now all contentable, contented is,
The folds and banks are sleepy: and the wind
Saunters at will, too lazy to discern
What's yet contentable upon the earth.
The mingled movements leave the softening pool,
And waters that have poured together soon
Cease to unite, and sink. Spreads, where was fire,
A double warmth of half assuaged desire.
Where unicorns their doting muzzles laid,
With melting ice as dear is scarleted.
And the dull aches that pay them for their care
So faithful through the years, unheeded are
In seeming perfectness within the sphere.

But when the day dawned bare of bird aubade
And sodden taste, and sour, of middle age
Awoke him, turned he to survey his bride:
And found there still half-sleeping at his side
A crab where he had seen a maiden's hand,
A corpse decaying where her flesh had lain,
A bullock and a ram where had been loving.
He left the bed with a loud cry of loathing
And naked wandered through the chilly house.
'What is this anuby of love,' he said, 'what ruse
Eats me and cheats me out of joy? Too true
Is the old tale of Helen, that wise Zeus
Set up an image of her face in Troy:
And thinking it was she, that quaint decoy
Men fought for, while she hidden lived alone.'

The Virgin stirred upstairs in bed alone
And wearily awoke. 'Why celebrate
Weddings with Tornaboda in their wake?'
She sighed, 'What have I married? Not a man,
But a menagerie of different men.'
She cried herself to sleep again: he walked: the sun
Rose, and set: and a whole month was gone.
Then through the twilight rose a yellow gloom.
Loxias save us! Yet another moon?

Libra, or,
The Scales

Publius Aemilius Hadrianus
Publius Aemilius Hadrianus Graeculus
Is in the evenings to be seen in a first class carriage
In the mornings deals with branch office correspondence in all parts
    of the world.

His policy slogan is Pax Romana
Employed to revive Greek Culture——
The shrine of Poseidôn Hippias is locked with wool
Our age respects the god by locking it with a Roman wall.

Were the Greeks better men than we?
He believes in the Roman Empire, bareheaded
In the rights of property he believes, according to Ratio.
In some ways the Greeks were better men than we.

He owns a collection of antiquities
A collection of antiquities he also possesses:
His possession not prætorian, but legal,
His ownership Roman.

More correctly, he owns the right to these
The right to these he also possesses:
But he owns the right of possession
And possesses the right of ownership.

If so, possession is governed by ownership
And ownership can be possessed:
Which is absurd.
Ask any prætor.

Inasmuch as he enunciates Pax Romana
He must hold himself slave to Lex Romana.

By torchlight he has seen his own shadow
But the stars were dim: in Athens.
He has seen all the visible stars,
But lost his own light: in the Sabine Hills.

In this beloved Athens was a statue of Antinous
Which he possessed, for he could forbid others access:
Which he owned, for none had a better right than he:
In this beloved Athens was his statue of Antinous.

Athens he owned: but did he possess it?
Absent, he had animus: but its governor had corpus.
Present, he had corpus also: but its governor also had animus.
The governor, though responsible, did not represent him.

Absent, if he had ownership, he had no possession.
Did he have ownership, there?
He was a stranger when he went there:
The very past had better right than he.

Athens was owned by the past.
If present he did not own it, neither could he absent:
The Emperor of the World
Neither owned nor possessed his favourite city.

Is not the past incorporeal?
An incorporeal is no owner.
The past of Athens is its present people.
They own Athens.

Light dawns.

We are confusing human law with divine.

One city of Athens is a fungible thing,

The other a thing religious, relict to the gods of souls dead.

But what is fungible Athens?

A city of trams and hotels, drains, taxes on eatables,

Annual revenue, unmanured soil, and upkeep of ancient monuments.

This is not his, but the governor's, Athens.

And now, as it were, the light turns green:

For Antinous also is a thing of divine right,

A thing sacred by authority of the Roman people:

And a thing of divine right is the goods of nobody.

His sacred friend, his city and of the gods,

He owns neither: this is what comes of thinking.

Let us touch the scales again,

That they poise serenely balancing.

What possession is, nobody knows,

Ownership's little idiot brother: but somewhere between

The possibility of being dispossessed

And the impossibility of being dispossessed.

More than detention, less than dominion,
Relative to dominion,
But, relatively to detention, absolute.
Which is absurd.

As a right, it is a question of fact:
As a fact, it cannot be called continuous, i.e., real,
Without reference to right.
Which is absurd.

It is contradictory
And it is simple:
But one man at a time cannot see its simplicity:
Which also is absurd.

A servant taking my cloak to the tailor
Has all evidences of possession, but not possession,
Which the law does not give him
Because he has not got it.

But to the thief who steals it,
The law gives unlawful possession lawfully:
The law balances the fact.
Balance abides our king.

Awkward, worthless, unintelligible, these
We go on making in order to obey them:
But for the sake of the Pax Romana,
Which is not absurd but reasonable.

In the corner of the compartment
Wherein twenty-four profiles of expressionless noses
Bob up and down like dancers' knees,
From an advertisement square, sulkily, a ram stares.

In an oblong advertisement above, rounded on the roof curve,
A bent moon dips down to its horns in false perspective.
Why does he feel he has seen that before?
Why does the bend seem so important?

Not because the Roman Empire needs advertisement:
It is known the wide world over.
Though advertisements are reasonable.
All monuments are reasonable.

No supernumerary emotions to appear on parade.
This impersonal cosmos by ideas was created:
By personalities it is obscured,
Or intensified to unmilitary degrees.

Emotions may have preserved Poseidôn Hippios
But emotions snap wool.
A wall is rational and reliable
To preserve Poseidôn Hippios.

Reason is a weight apparatus
Induction and exhaust
Influences come up for judgment
Two minutes apart like trains in a tube.

Bull bellows, lion plunges back to jungle:
Twin dies, virgin offers herself
Sideways creeps crab,
But scales are firm.

Halfway between summer and winter we poise in fall of leaves
Halfway between fidelity and adultery we enjoy our neutral dreams
But like a yellow light in a tunnel not yet reached
The thistlefinch repeats his twittering track:

    little soul, little flirting,
       little perverse one,
           guest and companion of the body,
               where are you off to now?

little wan one, firm one,
little exposed one,

.   .   .   .   .

and never make fun of me again?

Scorpio, or, The Scorpion

Now as the farmer sits at his accounts
Reviewing fleeces neath deciduous beeches
And notes in red contented ink
Net profits of his quite impossible serenity;
As graded apples marketably beautiful
Into the bushel-baskets sink
And trussed hay to the tin roof reaches,
And where red tiles through darkening trees are reared
A whole year's work is sold in sacks of meal;
Now suddenly running
Drops like a sprig
Of oak in a gale on the neck
The little wriggler,
Vindictive-legged cunning,
Drops like a fleck
Of blood on a finger ring
Crooking his sting.

It wriggles and stops,

Wriggles and turns

Through copper ferns

Through stubble of crops

Into the garden of his most impossible serenity.

Chrysanthemums

Wilt in alarm

As dangerous comes

Its arching arm

A probable harm

Nearer to his impossible serenity.

Brambles turn sour

Berries crinkle

All fruits,

Every flower,

All roots wrinkle:

The trees' atour

Lapses, and the power

Of his impossible serenity

Collapses.

The scorpion poison grips, its patterns spread

Like wine that trickling on a dusty floor

Hence and thence makes pellets and canals.

Asphodel, improbable, beside the river bed

Is found rank ramsons with a garlic smell.

And cider in a dirty cask, lovelike, turns vinegar.

Where had been pears and pippins, is a row of rotten balls,

Globes of mundungus, faced with foul fungus,

And locusts swarm to make the end complete.

The last bee disembowelled waves its dislocated feet.

Diseased the last elm falls, and with it falls

The indistinct last glint of Dionysus

Lysius.

Earth is with scorpions like spiders hung.

From every tile and brick they flick

Like leaping twisting mixing flies on dung.

A pretty virgin makes a pretty shrew,

As those no longer virgins also do,

Because they are no longer so, or else because they are.

The fracasado, self-considering as from far,

By force of self-perverted scales

Pities himself for impotence, and rails

Oftener therefore: more he pities, more he fails.

The scolding wife drives man to keep a scolding whore:

If either dies, he grieves because she scolds no more,

And scorns the other still because she scolds.

The man whose one wife makes him ten cuckolds

Wishes the girl were plain: she finds no joys
In playing with her multiplicated boys,
Wishes herself plain too, to find her joy in one. Whose wife
Is dutiful and bashful all her life
Thinks he would be happier if she were loved by other men.
Surely some wit usurps the throne of Cypris, when
Woman so seems what never woman was,
For man to caper to as man should not.
The golden mean is not.

The man of business bonded to his trade
Postpones his culture till his fortune has been made.
The cultured man to realize his will
Can find no means, nor wherewithal to touch
His learning, since his culture costs too much.
Reformers, visionaries, poets, other such,
Because their vision real is, too sane their wit,
The multitude they seek to benefit
Lunatic calls them: and although they spurn
Others' opinions, lunatic for lack of heed they turn,
Parodying their visions of perfection.
The land, too stupid to desire a change,
Too lazy for that mental insurrection,
Yet knowing their salvation lies
In broader education,

Like cats enough uneasy to surmise
They have the mange,
Further enlightenment refuses
And its chief men accuses
Of unenlightenment,
With consequent
Stagnation.

Over its losses
Autumn its mosses
Draws: the dormice go to sleep.
In the shorter afternoons
Determined to forget, the caterpillars crawl
Into the weak oblivion of cocoons.
To easier life the coward birds have all
Flown from the towns and woods and pools:
But some remain at large, poor ignorant fools.
The bats are wiser, who hang upside down,
Less crazily inverted than the town:
Snails in cement immure their sleepy souls:
Less mad, though timid, are the celibate
Ferns that abide the next arriving spring
To unroll fronds again, when warblers sing,
Meantime intelligently hibernate,
And delicately,
Up to date.

But we as leaves evacuate a lime
Cannot deceive ourselves nor bide our time:
Forced to retire by buds that seize our place,
Self-superannuated, in disgrace,
Know but too well that what we most deride
In others is the poison on our side,
Stung by the poison we ourselves put up
Ourselves the poisoned cup
We give our intellectual pride
To sup.

A scorpion drops from a unicorn's nape
Into the virgin's lap.
A scorpion drops from blond Xanthippê's tongue
And Socratês though he have wrung
A whole night's liquor from a score kulixes
And sadly his wine mixes,
Drinking all below the table,
Wanders, constitutionally unable
To drink himself unwise.
Yes, even him approaching now to weigh these things
The scorpion stings.

This belt of fretted stars that so promiscuously plays
Upon our eyes, we learn to name them all,

Picking our favourites out like horses in a race.

But now their steady passages recall

How, geared to the years,

They tick our lives out: and we cease to see

Much hope in false futurity:

Instead we falsify stars that have been

With promise that we alter since those stars,

Raising reality

Not in what we see,

Nor in what meteors there yet may be,

But in fixed stars we would we once had seen.

Sagittarius, or, The Archer

As a corpse face in shadow of a shrub
Would gleam, pale, bruised, and half invisible,
So hangs the moon, gibbous, and no more subdivisible.
We go no farther thus.
                            But come with me,
Old Berkeley, join our Lion-Scales-Virginity
In search without extension of triangularity.
News is, in Space-Time Einstein got
Two simultaneous events and unconnected
Which, he discovered, one pure triangle erected.
Is this our quest? We know that it is not.
Come, for the sky is crisp with crystal prisms,
The ground is bouldered o'er with cataclysms.
Knee-high the air is dense with ghostly hills
And ghostly parapets and plains too cool,
Flat bulky floors of cottonwool
And gaps in space that spatial fluid fills.

This grey-white city grown of pendent curves

Whose corners fold, whose copingstones are domes,

Bulging façades with pores like honeycombs

And every wall as womb to neighbour serves,

Tramp we, our calves nakedly its foundations

Piercing, as the keelskins of canoes.

On not a fathom's half of lucid air

Opaque the clustered floatages do cruise

Each saturating, bumping, drifting everywhere.

As our cold feet the empty bottom tread,

So above rounded roofs our triple head

Counts unobstructed glintings in the sky:

Silver Orion watching angrily

The quiet spinning of the Pleiades

Like nuns at home: while in the Western seas

Her blue hull Vega steers without farewell.

Resolute Sirius at the warrior's feet

Stares his loud wealth, which from a higher street

Procyon copies: caught in his own spell

The wizard Algol dying on the hill

With weakened grip has fallen from his net,

But one strand stretches to suspend him yet.

The mists float liquid, but the sky is still,

A city on a city laid. We come

Resignedly, and reverently, dumb

Our quarry in its sanctuary to find.

Tauten our mind.

Our quarry in its sanctuary sleeps

As yet: as yet no raping daylight creeps

Brutally on its quest: nor stops the owl

Dashing destroyer-like with foghorn howl.

We bruise our feet because no vision is,

And shut our eyes along the precipice.

The pools we plunge in through the ground mist splash

Spurting in stars that vanish as they flash:

The molehills lift us under the thick sheet:

And if in spaces we may clearings meet

They serve but to disclose a further fog.

Night is the end, and mist the epilogue.

Rhyming our pathway falters. On the banks

Of pale wool widen flanks of paler waves

Like moonlit headstones over moonlit graves,

And purpose gathers on those widening flanks.

Up in the citadel the windows cease

To glint metallic: in the darker west

Where Vega on the horizon long has pressed,

Glimmer the far departing Pleiades,

And wan Orion bows too to depart.

The eastern constellations like a hart

Seen mottled betwixt leaves of forest trees,

Dappling fade into the siccate sky,
But white and stedfast as they pass him by
His destined note the Morning Planet frees.

Come let us draw our bows. The quarry springs
Alarmed from cover: at whose noisy break
A thousand pigeons swift on squeaky wings
Flood, like the firmament become awake,
Across this glade. Magpies and startled rails
Squawk: and the rabbits ricochet their tails
White-tufted. Suddenly and far away
Not dawndumb yet the bittern in the marsh
Booms: and the corbies make the morning harsh.
In the mute suburbs at the dawn of day
Bird bands in garden bandstands make all gay,
Misselthrush, throstle, blackbird, and redbreast,
And ladies to newspapers write to say
Which of the pretty songsters they like best,
When in their soft beds, proud to be awake,
They hear sweet nature from her slumber break.
But here there is no comfort and no light.
A dull expansion, dawn makes our earth bare
Of cover. We have trodden down the night,
Now its successor fronts us. The white air
Shudders. Nothing is still. Contempt

Echoes from rocks. Aye, for our cowardice
Us from the blame who would not hold exempt,
Who alone braved the fog-made precipice?
What though we shut our eyes? Come, let us draw.
That little triple speck of dark you saw
Flung like a petal from the blossoming east,
That be our mark. Aim at the Morning Star,
Aim at the mists that yet too thick are pieced,
Aim where you will, so you stand where you are.
For thus, for thus. . . .
                    But Dawn comes meaningless.
Of all this purpose can we make nought wise?
Will nothing follow nights of nothingness?
Mists take the bird. The archer none the less
Shoots, and the arrow flies.

Capricornus, or, The Goat

Supervises over the teatable our voluble hostess

The passing round of titterings and toasties.

Her glass-eyed friends, confidence's make-and-breaks,

Give each in series gobbets of another's cakes.

Dough drips into their tight triangular shoes.

Their mouths give vent to evil-smelling news

Keep their minds pure, make mental products crisper,

With speaking eyeball rolls and the not too improper whisper.

Fawn-eyed, the daughter, a gossip apprentice,

Festoons gilt malice on her unmalicious twenties.

Holiday smarmed the manureminded ephebus

Sees in every skirt lubricity's rebus.

Sex is their unknown god, with neither purity nor pox,

To whom they genuflect whenever they enjoy their shocks.

A little of everything, is the note they strike,

The only limitation, what they think they do not like.

Always they suffer inexpressible injustices,

Making their own beds, these amateur Procrusteses,

But expect their maids to lie in them. The middle classes

Must have some defence against the vulgar masses.

They have no use for idle gossips that scarify:

But in their own leisure get together to verify

Rumours of rationalists, use of contraceptives,

Probable bastards, hope of their proving defectives

(Details being perquisites of good detectives).

This of course for the parish's sake. These long nose weevils

Seek knowledge of others', as expression of their own, evils:

And naught escapes being twisted and messed,

Their own souls included, on matters of interest.

Ignorant, superficial, malignant, self-deceived,

Ashamed to bear, but proud to be bereaved,

Devoted to truth's medals, but dismayed to see its flesh——

Babies are born to them in prams and crêches.

Lip-honouring peace, by their indignant whispers

Others they desecrate, their own insure, in their smug vespers.

At mattins for their own sins pray to be forgiven,

Revelling in others while walking home from heaven.

Martyrlike suffer for transgressions of the parish,

Or say they do, particularly the most garish.

But humbly at their bedside never hope that Jesus has destroyed

Others' misfortunes wholly, lest themselves be unemployed.
Such and so blasting are their faded Joys
Which Time, nor Sickness, never quite destroys.

Balder and balder every haircut
Cutting a caper as lewd as he dare cut,
Quasiphilosophically Capricorn carouses
Ill at ease in such respectable houses,
The disinherited soul of an atrabilious
Semi self-deprecating paterfamilias.
With many eyeglitters at women's legs in stockings
And at the schoolboys' furtive corybantic eyecockings,
His Bacchanalian belly he wobbles like a sack
With metaphysical justification as Dionysiac,
And ungenteel jokes undoubtedly due to his strabismus
Distorting even the quaint festivities of Christmas.
Remembering in the artificial afternoon
Old days when Pan his saxophonic tune
Under the ilex played, and how the figwood image
Nimbly swayed in nights of lustful scrimmage,
And how in pleased surprise he uttered several Eurekas
At finding the gross fungus Ithyphallus Impudicus.
With him his father's hair his father's scalp reveals
Commensurate, with scratching too much during silent meals,
With virgin's blood the holly on the wall

Drips. As from Druid branches fail to fall
Light, intense pearl juices from alabaster fitting,
The proper tight-drawn hostess cuts unwitting
Symbols of fertility from Christmas cake. All jollity
Is fastened down. Only innocent frivolity
Saturnalia is allowed in houses of good quality.

Tiddledywog. Meh, meh. The door bursts open wide
The Sunday china stands up horrified.
Tiddledywog. Meh, meh. All he has ever remembered
Bulges out like a plaster panel badly distempered.
Tiddledywog. Meh, membrum caprinum erexit:
Culpabat alia aliam, quia ipsa conspexit.
Tiddledywog. Tiddledywog. Tiddledywog.
First he puts under the mat Persian cat and Pekinese dog.
Then the tables' and chairbacks' torselling
Smashes, and piles on potsherds of Worcester porcelain.
Tiddledywog. Tiddledywog. Forefeet dangling like clappers
Dancing about he grips the frightened flapper's
Flaxen coils, throws to the ground and violates her.
Which done she becomes he: he hates her,
And turning on the boy, knocks his eyes out,
Strips him, and using sinewy tail as a knout
Flogs the boy till he eddies and faints. And the mother faints,
Whom Capricorn props up upon the chintz

And bathing her forehead with cold milk and tea
Reverses coldnesses that used to be.
But when she recovers, recovers himself and batters
The woman to death. This seems to mend matters.
Next pausing somewhat incommoded by his toils,
The carpets, cushions, colour schemes he soils.
Last in fierce memory of dislocate desire
The house itself he dislocates with fire.
Scatters the redhot imitation coals
Over this mortuary of human souls.
The imitation furniture goes up in smoke
And well fired china serves as admirable coke.
Like wood distilled that dribbles clammily
Oozes the ectoplasm of his burning family.
Various vermicular disseminations
Germinating from his character's past emanations,
Wriggle until he tramples them. This action
Causes him an electric satisfaction.
But as he leaves the drawing-room for the servants' hall
To seize the housemaid ere the whole place fall
He, bleating with dismay, or recognition rather,
Finds himself facing himself as his own father.
Incestuous terror tempts him to do patricide:
But this he cannot, lest it turn out suicide:
So forfeiting this chance of lovely pain,

Since man once killed can not have joy of killing self again,
And since the air is gradually overheating,
With slight discomfort in his merry bleating,
A muffler from the hall veiling him from being stark,
He leaves the house to meditate, quite decent, in the Park.

Attend the coda. Hardly out he passes
Ere the charred, smashed, cadaverous wilting masses,
Shape back to chintz and gilded wood and scones.
The ancient house of Capricorn & Sons
Stands unassailable in statu quo,
Unconscious of the wiles of wurrico.
Immaculate the virgin hopes her stare
Has an enlightened but offended air:
The boy unscarred eyes still the cakes and knees
Smiling as sticky as the things he sees:
The hostess volubly goes prattling on
Deadly and regular as Gatling gun:
With spurious teeth and with triangular feet
The friends tread on each other's corns and eat:
While Capricorn, morose from losing od,
Defends the Empire and the Will of God.

Aquarius, or,
The Water-Carrier

'When I was young, I was sad because I was not wise:
Now I am sad, being neither wise nor young.
The butchers slew the ox to save for Zeus their mysteries:
The axe, the knife, though wiped in water, far they flung
And hastened with souls tightly shut as were their eyes.

I was the water-carrier and the victim I,
Who slew myself to hide myself from shame.
Men sought me to rebuke my irresponsibility:
But I, who never comprehended half the game
I played, hid self in anonymity.

Now these white hairs have named me. Three score years
Of shapes remembered isolate my round of things.
Who now remains to diamond my wine and tears
With company? This dated laughter of my making rings
Empty on an auditorium void of ears.

'Tis long since the finch piped his barren pleasant song:
And since the blackthorn whipped its purple veins to snow.
Youth tried the valueless debates of right and wrong:
That miracle also died: so very long ago,
'Tis scarcely worth the pain of wondering how long.

We heard the stars, each month a chiming one,
Making carillons without tune or time.
Each miracle died. Each month impulsively the sun
Worked on from paradigm to paradigm.
'Tis hardly worth the pain of viewing what is done.'

The water-carrier at the rusty pump
Leans on the handle that she cannot move
Crying, there must be ice within the sump.
But we, too late, compel ourselves to prove
The rust that could not leaven the whole lump.

'But why thus, starless, people this inferior abyss
With shades of girls we loved, or gypsies we might fear?
No problem solveth such parenthesis:
If there is none to stand on trial near,
Why people this incomprehensible abyss?'

The winter sun sets on the reddened boles
Of trees outstanding from the centuries.
The moon that mirrors our ancestral souls
Is faint with failure and with sophistries
In winter pain that canopies the poles.

The moon is darkened and the sun is low.
Yet makes the water-carrier, as she works
Demurely at the rusty pump, much understanding flow
Of days when oil is loose and summer lurks
Aptly. But who she is the watcher does not know.

Blinded his meadowy eyes to eyes of hers,
His own face laden now with frosted beard
Of winter, like the frosted pile of firs
He suffered winter from: now three score yeared
Can find no kinship in his daughter's crucifiers.

Her eyes are green as meadows bright with golden flowers,
Her face like cuckoo flower pales,
Her shoulders answer with their secret powers
Resilient as daffodils in gales
The changing pressure of the months and hours.

Naiad-born with glad emphatic glances
Foots she the measure tapping with her foot:
Gaily a minuet with death she dances
Who echoes silently, and cannot put
Her merriment to silence, nor advances.

Yes, gay she fronts him: yes, she humours him:
With due obedience she bows demurely:
Unfrightened by his aspect grim
The ropes with steady hands she holds securely
Expecting open-eyed his senile change of whim.

The slanting sunlight on the garden path
Gilds her with patience. As his stricken days
Upbraid the imagined ruin of his secret garth
Still copper bracken in the russet rays
Stands orderly and trim as a swept hearth.

The minuet ends. The music is played wrong
And sad. The hidden clustered angels spread
Their silver wings, like memories of willow-warbler's song,
And vanish homeward to the long neglected dead.
So long ago the sacrifice was done. How long ago? How long?

She blames the butchers and the butchers blame the instruments
Which lie blood-varnished in the public dust.
Revive no memories of guilt and innocence!
What caused cessation was encroaching rust
Itself cessation's legal consequence.

The ten times buckled belt turns. The machine
Once dislocated, readjusted, plays
Retarded. But accepted is the scene
By us, too foreign to be daunted by dismays,
Too native still to make ourselves serene.

Grey in the evening are the paths and trees:
With little care we go indoors to leave them.
With little worth by contrast shone our coronals of ease
Although perplexedly we came to weave them,
Our gay designs, hard skills, austere perplexities.

The unknown maiden rests. The judges rest.
We are too near the namelessness to care
How she should be identified or be addressed.
The sun leads out, and we shall follow, where
What matter? There is nothing in this breast.

Who tried to consecrate the knife and axe?—Who sharpened them?
—Who took them to the priest?—Who made them then unholy?——
They fouled themselves: man is a stratagem
Used by subsisting forces. We are wholly
Unable to discriminate twixt anathem and catathem.

'Then throw them in the sea as deodands:
This does not satisfy, but it will pass.' So they adjudge,
Hurrying anxiously to weightier demands.
And home the jury dutifully through the winter trudge.
But we go journeying with less empty hands,

All of us, consciousness, alliances and quarrels,
Warped, but with wisdom battering the warps,
Normals, tuberculars, megalophrons, plethorals,
A hundred bodies in a single corpse,
Ten signs reflecting ten discordant morals.

Whence sound these chords of wood and violin?
A swallow measure tilts upon the air,
As a mole's fur is soft upon the skin,
So delicate, so warm, so debonair,
And again ay the harmonies begin.

Again our dancers tap their minuet,
Which in the next room merrily the sun
Joins: till our music meets the boundary set,
And stops capricious as it was begun.
This, darkness follows. But it ends not yet.

Pisces, or, The Fishes

For a doxology there is yet to sing:
For still the Zodiac, like a skylark's wing,
Flutters, although man's zeal be all paid down.
Still, though without a telescoped renown,
Jumps the uncharted jumble of the stars:
Still from existence warehouse see it send
The metanairesis beyond the end:
And still the engine, untransmitting, sucks
Cyclic serial zeniths from the flux,
Where like eccentric shadows on a wall
The periodic planets rise and fall.

The fishes in the globe of time and space
Slide round to bear the thrusting of the race
And each nose touches, as the night goes on,
The quivering tail-fin of the former one.

The stars are ugly: we with hands aware
Group them in wisps of Berenice's hair,
Though fingers that must falter ere the end
Corona's battered circlet cannot mend,
Nor faulty labyrinths of ear denote
In what dimensions may these fishes float.
Yet float they do and move their yearly lap
Regardless of achievement and mishap,
While to the stars that change not from their birth
Ecliptic planets lend successive worth.
First Jupiter, a soldier home from war,
Treads the thin purple carpet to the door.
All his adventures in the hall he tells,
How he surprised the sleeping sentinels,
Murdered a tyrant, raped a richer gold,
And burned a thousand foemen in a hold.
But ere he ends, he turns to disappear
And leaves the fishes circling the sphere.

Next with a tilting change of human mode
Arrives the yellow Uranus at node.
Confusion riots. Undertones of passion
Burst into faiths that minister to fashion.
Muses malignant working by lampoons
The fluted columns alter to gadroons,

Or to view Heaven's qualities and Hell's
All columns exorcise from dirty cells.
But what the influence that starts their phlegm?
The ghost of Jupiter obsesses them.
Whatever mystery they worship most,
The very genius of them is a ghost,
A ghost that vanishes and as they fear
Makes Uranus as well to disappear
And leave the fishes circling the sphere.

Third on the journey, by the first two freed,
Lumbers tired Saturn at pedestrian speed.
The lazy poets meet him. Journalist bards
Finish their cigarettes and games of cards
And follow if they wish (There is no hurry):
Or if not ready yet, they do not worry.
For though they call discursive and extraneous
All poetry that is not instantaneous,
The new Augustans never are in haste.
Their bitter absinthe is too good to waste.
But planets cannot stop. And Time impugns
The most Augustan Sunday afternoons.
Saturn abducts, ere scarcely he alights,
His one-verse-contemplating satellites,

And with the yellow-eyed, and with the sere,
He sweeps the board of dignitaries clear,
And leaves the fishes circling the sphere.

Now Neptune follows, and his follower, Mars.
Parabolas of planets mid the stars
Shoot, dip and fall, like rockets fired in turn.
And with the notes of platinum they burn,
Notes too refined to reach our faulty ear,
Illume the fishes circling the sphere,
In each reflected as its lustre dips
That of the one it cannot quite eclipse.
But one remains, Winter and Summer through,
A double impulse, as it had been two.
Eve calls if Hesper, Dawn the Morning Star,
These two appearances one vision are.
Female or male, midnight or afternoon,
Who dockets the companion of the moon?
Who understands the total that is told
Rich or castrated, frenzied or controlled,
Pagan or Puritan, Awareness, Mind,
Which bears all oppositions in its kind,
Wherewith all other planets' faces hang
Conjunct, in unity of Yin and Yang?

He knows who watches and survives the rout.

For clustered lights can never be put out,

But though the separate scintillants decay

The sum of them, once realized, must stay.

This is the mystery that has been said

Of two or three together gathered:

No muddy vesture, and no choking stoles,

Deafen such harmony in immortal souls.

The wise, although they suffer from the Crab,

Trusting in Man, but not in astrolab,

Abandon cold accounts of gain and cost.

So all is reconciled and nothing lost:

And what had failed the hard material need

A larger view discovers to succeed.

We eschew nothing, but are poets still,

And so shall prosper poetwise, until

Some rhomboid planet, purple or maroon,

Call man to island man in a balloon,

Or give the poem of redintegration

To some souled, parallel epipedal crustacean:

And spiralling that hypothetic gear

Still go the fishes circling the sphere.

But I, who started with the lowest sun,

See its course low again as I have done.

Winter records, halfway, in howling words
Farewell or welcome to the foreign birds,
So I the seasons, as they each careen
And scour themselves across the wrangling scene.
I use the stars as wisely as I can
With migrant man as faith to migrant man.

Author's Notes

ARIES: The sampler of which use is here made is in the possession of John Fothergill, of the Spreadeagle, Thame. The first four lines are a translation, and the last couplet an emendation, of lines 28–31 of the poem ERASTES, attributed to Theocritus, but kept apart as suspect by Wilamowitz in the Oxford Text of the Greek Bucolic Poets. The emendation is in a spirit characteristic of the Ram: for a literal translation of the passage is:

> The rose is fair, and Time it withereth.
> The violet fair in spring. It quickly ages.
> White the lily: withers, once 'tis shed.
> And Snow is white: melts, where it had been frozen.
> And beautiful, a youth's beauty: but it lasts not long.

TAURUS: Lines 1–4. A Greek folksong to Dionysus. J. M. Edmonds in his Lyra Graeca adds the note: 'Pausanias goes on to tell of the miraculous filling of sealed winejars overnight, which took place at the festival: in this very ancient invocation D. is still a "hero" and a bull.'

Lines 32–9 and 105–8. These passages do not attempt to reproduce the song of a goldfinch, which is too liquid and quick for English words, or indeed for any except possibly Greek words. They merely suggest it, and have small syntactical sense.

Lines 61 et seq. The ceremony of the Bull murder at the Athenian Dipolia appearing here and in AQUARIUS is described in *The Golden Bough*. In Classical times it was regarded as out of date.

CANCER: Lines 102, etc. Miser Catulle, desinas ineptire. English scazons.

LIBRA: Line 34. The doctrine of Paulus. An anachronism.

Last lines. Animula, vagula, blandula. Hadrian's lyric.

A Note on the Text

This edition of *The Ecliptic* is based on the edition published by Faber & Faber Limited in 1930. The text has been checked for accuracy against other versions of the poem: a manuscript in the Poetry Collection at SUNY-Buffalo, a typescript at the Beinecke Rare Book and Manuscript Library at Yale University, and a publication of "Leo" in *The Criterion* volume IX, number 37 (July 1930). Some corrections have been made accordingly. In a few instances, commas and apostrophes have been introduced for clarity.

Afterword

Born in the West London suburb of Ealing to Scottish parents in 1903, Joseph Gordon Macleod was educated at Balliol College, Oxford, where he qualified as a barrister but turned away from a career in law and toward a life in the arts. Before investing himself fully in the theater, as he later would, Macleod devoted his intellectual energies first to literary criticism and then to poetry. *Beauty and the Beast*, a volume of formally innovative criticism, was published by Chatto & Windus in Britain in 1927 and by Viking Press in the United States the following year. During the summer of 1928 Macleod composed *The Ecliptic*, a poem ambitious not only in length but scope and intensity. After sharing an early draft with Basil Bunting, Macleod wrote to Ezra Pound in a letter dated 11 December 1929:

> Bunting also says that he asked you to read the poem I wrote last summer, + you have consented. This is very courteous of you, for I hear you read little new stuff (and wish I could do the same). The MS proper is at the moment being considered by Virginia Woolf for the Hogarth Press: but if you wouldn't mind a carbon copy—(quite legible but rather untidy) I would be delighted to send it to you.

The following spring, Bunting reported to Pound on his first meeting with the young poet: "Macleod proved rather Oxfordy. Bloomsbury, but decidedly likeable." More substantively, both Pound and Bunting were deeply impressed with the complex structure of *The Ecliptic*. The poem offers the narrative of a single consciousness in twelve parts, each of which corresponds to one of twelve constellations in the Western zodiac. It begins with Aries and closes with Pisces, moving from birth to death, with each section conveying a mood or quality specific to its phase of life and corresponding astrological sign. For his part, Pound was so taken by the architecture of the poem that in a letter to Louis Zukofsky, he wrote, "Have you seen J. G. Macleod's *Ecliptic*? I mention only to show the 'need' being felt for longer poems built on a plan."

At Pound's encouragement, T. S. Eliot accepted the poem for Faber & Faber, where it was published in 1930 as part of a series of emerging poets that included Philip Graves and W. H. Auden. From the outset, *The Ecliptic* has enjoyed a number of distinguished readers, including not only Pound and Bunting, but Zukofsky, Kenneth Rexroth, Hugh MacDiarmid, Delmore Schwartz, and J. H. Prynne. In the April 1931 issue of *Poetry* magazine, the editor-in-chief Morton Dauwen Zabel framed Macleod as part of a cultural renaissance in the United Kingdom, a new "Dawn in Britain" among poets; he exuberantly praised *The Ecliptic* as a work of "compelling originality and technical subtlety." The following year, in the February issue of *Poetry* on British verse, Bunting boldly remarked that, upon its publication, *"The Ecliptic* interested me more than any new thing since *The Waste Land."*

Originally arranged by Pound to follow on the heels of the well-known Objectivist issue of *Poetry* edited by Zukofsky, the British issue had far less impact and influence. Edited in part by Bunting, it showcased an unusually uneven constellation of poems from Cecil Day Lewis, the minor Scottish poet J. J. Adams, Macleod, and Bunting himself, as well as commentaries from Allen Tate on Aldous Huxley, Bunting on Adams and Macleod, and other critical remarks on poets associated with the Auden circle. In a letter to Pound dated 6 November 1930, Zukofsky had expressed a clear desire to draw Macleod into the fold of the Objectivist issue: "I don't see why—Eng. issue be damned—why I shouldn't get Macleod & J. J. Adams and other Ingles if I can get 'em—and *if* they're good." But against Zukofsky's interest, Macleod was relegated to the less coherent and less successful British issue, to which he contributed an excerpt from a new poem, *Foray of Centaurs*. Baroque and intellectually opaque, *Foray of Centaurs* was soon after turned down by Faber & Faber. Having failed to find a publisher for his second major poetic effort, Macleod began to focus his attention more intensely on his work in theater.

From 1930 through the onset of the Second World War, the poet served under director Terence Gray as an actor and producer at the Cambridge Festival Theatre, which he would eventually come to direct himself from 1933 to 1936. As Macleod recalls in his memoir *The Actor's Right to Act* (1981), it was in the Cambridge Festival Theatre that he embraced revolutionary socialism. While performing stage work, he was electrocuted and—after hanging unconscious from a curtain—experienced a political epiphany. That this political awakening occurred, according to Macleod, while laboring for the theater offers us a sense of how he understood the relation between culture and politics. His newfound commitment led to a brief political career, first as chairman of the Huntingdonshire Divisional Labour Party, and then as a candidate for parliament. But when he failed to gain election, he took a job reading news for the BBC, a post he held from 1938 until the end of the war. His voice can be heard in *Listen to Britain* (1942), a war-effort montage directed for the British Ministry of Information's Crown Film Unit by documentary filmmaker Humphrey Jennings, a friend Macleod knew from the Cambridge Festival Theatre. By war's end, Macleod moved to Glasgow to serve from 1945–47 as director of Scottish National Film Studios, an enterprise that, despite widespread anticipation in the national press, produced only one short film on road safety.

While engaged in these diverse activities from the late 1930s through the early 1940s, Macleod produced an overwhelming body of writing in a number of different genres: poetry, literary criticism, music criticism, drama, and theater history. Trips to the U.S.S.R. during the forties yielded several significant books of theater criticism, including *The New Soviet Theatre* (1943) and *A Soviet Theatre Sketchbook* (1951). But if this was an industrious period in Macleod's intellectual life, it was also a conflicted one. In reaction to the rich formal innovation that characterizes early efforts such as *The Ecliptic*, Macleod began publishing dramatic poetry under the pseudonym Adam Drinan, a defiantly parochial Scottish persona whose works included *The Cove* (1940), *The Men of the Rocks* (1942), and *Women of the Happy Island* (1944).

Unlike fellow Scotsman, poet, and activist Hugh MacDiarmid, who declared in *A Drunk Man Looks at Thistle* (1926), "I'll ha'e nae hauf-way hoose, but aye be whaur / Extremes meet," Macleod cleanly compartmentalizes his extremes. We see this most clearly in the split between Joseph Gordon Macleod, the cosmopolitan modernist Pound found so intriguing, and Adam Drinan, the decidedly populist poet of the Scottish Renaissance concerned with the voices, folk traditions, and history of the Highlands. Macleod does not cease writing and publishing under his own name once the poet Adam Drinan emerges; the cultural interests of the two personae are simply kept separate from one another. The sharpest instance of this simultaneity occurs in *The New British Poets* edited by Kenneth Rexroth. Published by New Directions in 1956, this anthology includes poetry from both Macleod and Drinan without offering any evidence to suggest these two poets are in fact one and the same or that Rexroth knew any better. Public ignorance regarding Macleod's pseudonym was so thorough that MacDiarmid, writing in 1953, referred to the mystery surrounding Drinan's elusive identity as "one of the best preserved secrets of the contemporary literary world."

Of course, the Drinan work coincides with Macleod's devoted attention to Soviet theater during the 1940s, and both reflect his ongoing interest in communal art and Marxist politics. From the 1950s onward Macleod further pursued his commitment to theater and performance, with publications that included *Piccola Storia del Teatro Britannico* (1958), *The Sisters d'Aranyi* (1969), and *The Actor's Right to Act* (1981). In 1955 Macleod moved to Florence, Italy, where he lived out the rest of his years. Far from Scotland and its concerns, the Drinan work waned; Macleod published a final sequence of verse, *An Old Olive Tree* (1971), under his own name. At his death in 1984, he left a broad and generative body of work, one that reflects his twin affinities for poetry and theater, poiesis and performance.

Richard Owens